Friendly Street
NEW POETS 11

Friendly Street
NEW POETS 11

low background noise • Cameron Fuller

words free • Simone G Matthews

jars of artefacts • Rachel Manning

Friendly Street Poets

Wakefield Press

Friendly Street Poets Incorporated
in association with
Wakefield Press
1 The Parade West
Kent Town
South Australia 5067

www.friendlystreetpoets.org.au
www.wakefieldpress.com.au

First published 2006

Cover artwork by Tom Moore
Cover design by Clinton Ellicott, Wakefield Press
Typeset by Ryan Paine, Wakefield Press
Printed and bound by Hyde Park Press, Adelaide

ISBN 1 86254 701 7

JamFactory Gallery represents Tom Moore. Many thanks to Tom,
and Debbie Pryor, Gallery Manager, www.jamfactory.com.au.

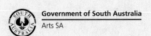 Friendly Street is supported by the
South Australian Government
through Arts South Australia.

 Wakefield Press thanks Fox Creek Wines
for their support.

Contents

low background noise

Cameron Fuller

Cameron Fuller was born on the shores of Lake Burley Griffin in Canberra. He has lived in Brisbane, Sydney and Cairns, but keeps returning to Adelaide, where he has done most of his living and writing. Having studied at five universities in three states, he holds a degree at the University of Queensland and has recently completed Honours in Professional Writing and Communication at the University of South Australia.

Acknowledgements

Some of these poems have appeared in
Southerly, Social Alternatives, Artstate and
My cat cannot have friends in Australia
(2004 Wollongong Poetry Workshop
Anthology), and one has
been broadcast on *PoeticA*.

Many thanks to Ioana Petrescu for her
editorial advice and generous encouragement;
to Jules Leigh Koch for his ongoing support;
and to Deb, Pete, Bet and Josie for everything.

Contents

my ungrammatical self

standing at the edge of a crowd
awkwardly   a dangling modifier   i am

among louder voices with perfect grammar
fit in where do i

a neanderthal at a literary event
there is only wine but me like beer

i approach someone holding a glass of red
adjectives grunt from my colloquial throat

and my faulty syntax
a silence leads into

unsure how to smoothly unsplit my infinitives
once they're printed in the minds of others

i wonder where my antecedent is
and look for an exit

quietly
into ellipsis
i slip

sometimes, meanings

sometimes i want to tear at the skin of a poem
    and see its heart beating underneath
sometimes i want to sweep through the clutter of words
    and watch meanings scatter to the corners of a page

sometimes i'll sit quietly
    as a poem yells until it's out of breath
sometimes i'm embarrassed
    when a poem whispers its deepest desires

sometimes a sign flashes above my head in red neon
       all types welcome
       the poem more difficult than a game of chess
     the poem thrusting its hips in the face of the reader
the poem confessing its secrets to strangers

sometimes i enter a poem
    and all i hear is white noise
but sometimes it's like waking
    to the smell of fresh bread and coffee

and sometimes a poem returns at night
       to find my dumb heart thumping a rhythm
     as vowels purr in the throat
    consonants pulsate on lips
and words float in the warm currents of the mind

Adelaide from a near distance

Driving through the hills at dusk,
we see at every curve a different angle of the city.
Our talk turns to carving a meaning from life:

you imagine the world beyond these hills;
I keep looking at the city, already sparkling
orange and white. The road is dark and full of turns,

and our words give way to laughter.
The broken radio dial stuck on easy-listening.
After an hour of Air Supply, Celine Dion, Reo Speedwagon . . .

we become delirious. We twist bad lines into even worse ones:
Our love soars over mountain tops – or at least Mount Lofty;
The moon glows just for you and me – and six billion others.

Life reduced to a three-minute love song,
we descend to the city, and soon, I know,
the street lights will wash over your face as you sleep.

And with the radio turned off, and the car humming quietly,
my eyes will turn between you and the road,
knowing our place in the world is clear for at least one more night.

Another lacklustre performance

Tonight
     as you line
          up those closet
               romantics and
                    put them out
                         of their misery –
                              as they pause by
                                   the ocean to see
                                        you in its tide, as
                                             they crave you like
                                                  chocolate – I will not
                                                       pity them like I pity
                                                            you. I will not trace
                                                                 your fuzzy outline as
                                                                      you move through that
                                                                           circular rising-and-falling
                                                                                narrative. I will not watch
                                                                                you loom over the city,
                                                                                glowing as if you've been
                                                                                given appearance money
                                                                                and a contract stating you'd
                                                                                be seen only through a soft
                                                                                lens. I know you're suffering
                                                                                from overexposure. I know
                                                                                you're having lunch with
                                                                                developers. I know even
                                                                           the poets who use you to
                                                                      silhouette their loneliness
                                                                 don't howl anymore. To-
                                                            night you're an aging
                                                       rock star. Tonight
                                                  the clouds can't hide
                                             your scars, craters,
                                        pock holes. Tonight
                                   you can't escape
                              the minds
                         of critics
                    dreaming
               up head-
lines.

Caravan park theory

Do not air dirty laundry
on the communal clothesline
warns a sign on the ablution block.
I look over at white sheets waving in the wind,
shake the sand from my board shorts
and mark with pegs a site of resistance.
Trying to evade surveillance,
I walk along the side streets,
past begging seagulls and onsite vans
flanked with crates of empty beer bottles.
Radios announce the soundtrack of summer
will once again be 'classic rock'.
But here, there's the rhythm and melody
of raised voices, slamming aluminium doors
and thongs slapping concrete.

A crowd gathers within a city
of silver-domed tents.
Their efficient use of space,
their ordered arrangement of lines
while queuing for food: faultless.
From the outskirts, they stare suspiciously
at my shanty tent – my Kmart holiday.

After unwinding their second home, a family settles in
to a routine. Mum reads an erotic short story
in a magazine. Dad lies on a deck chair, daydreaming
about licking beer flavoured ice cream
from his favourite swimsuit model's breasts.

Under pine trees, kids run across scattered needles
and through sprinklers, screaming
and soaking themselves in treated water.
At the van, Mum offers a towel,
Dad sends them to the kiosk for ice cream.
The nuclear family exploded long ago,
but its fragments are found
in caravan parks every summer.

The long afternoon
is a slow-cooking casserole –
all gristle and juice.
Bodies that glisten with sunscreen
move in and out of water as slow as the tide,
leaving only when the sun ushers them out.
The arrival of darkness
is signalled by the sizzle of barbecues
and mozzie zappers frying meat.
As voices float in the breeze,
the park finds its nightly rhythm
in the muffled crash and fizz
of waves, of bodies
curling under sheets.

sunset gelati

a swirl
            of apricot
                                    peach
                    mango
                                        and strawberry

        then   a   big   scoop   of   blueberry

First night in the snow

Leaving Spencer Street station, I look back to the grey footpaths where one man after another asked for change. Through the inner and outer suburbs, the hobby farms and the real ones, the rise above sea level is so gradual, I'm surprised by the white stuff on the ground. On the mountain, the more snow lumped on trees, the more I think of desert plains. Australia or Austria? A syllable missing, buried like a car in a blizzard.

In the village, a thick cloud stuck in the main street, the glow of pensions and chalets, and a room with a view. Crossing the street, snow crunching under boots, people smile and say 'Hi'. I walk past a lift machine, motionless under floodlights, towards a clock tower and the coloured neon of cafes. A door opens and I'm hit by a warm pocket of coffee and garlic. I ponder the cost of a meal and a room, and gaze out a window, astounded how quickly things can snowball. At this higher altitude, I wonder if being a tourist means forgetting certain realities – like the degree of difference between sinking into a couch by a fireplace and squatting in a damp warehouse, or the faces that know too well the streets that aren't as soft as snow.

Pretending I'm a traveller, not a tourist
Thailand

After leaving our *Lonely Planet*
in a cafe on Khao Sahn Road, we find ourselves
in a town near the Laotian border,
standing alone on cracked pavement,
liberated from the sight of westerners in sarongs.

By late afternoon, we're in a *tuk-tuk*,
heading for a temple. At the edge of town,
we begin to breathe smoke.
The driver points towards a bushfire –
the monsoon is late: *many cloud, no rain.*
A light film of ash coats our faces
as buffalo laze in rice fields
set against a swollen sun.

In the temple grounds,
children play soccer in dust.
We leave our boots at the entrance
where three sleeping dogs lie.
Inside, a huge golden Buddha
sits in darkness. At his feet,
incense sticks, dried flowers
and a bowl of mandarins
rest on a table draped in saffron cloth.
For a moment, we close our eyes,
but, weary from months of travelling,
do not find clarity. We notice
flakes of gold paint on the floor

and push handfuls of *baht*
into an empty donation box.

In the surrounding village, lanterns glow
around the teak houses
resting above the long reeds
of an oily river.
The last grains of sunlight
show an old man squatting
over a doorstep, and over him,
an old woman gliding
a pair of scissors through his hair.

Returning in darkness, we urge the night sky
to enlighten us. But there is no illumination
and no scent of moisture in the air.
Only feelings that don't translate
into 'craving', 'thirst' and 'desire'.
As lights appear in the distance,
we grasp at each transient moment,
knowing tomorrow will bring a new town
and a different perspective.

Amateur anthropology

I went into those countries,
    not unlike Malinowski:
  camera around my neck,
Europe in my pocket,
    Asia in my lungs.
  Each moment ready to shoot an image
I'd frame in my own culture.
    Each person observing my strangeness,
  keeping their findings to themselves.
Each town displaying signs of Western products.
    Each village appearing like an antique,
  showing the fingerprints of other cultures.
Each day a discovery
    revealing a layer of my self.
  Each night recording an urge to see people
refuse the lure of foreign currency
    and stay as timeless images in my mind:
  men steering elephants in the streets,
women bending over rice fields,
    families sleeping in single rooms,
  smiles from mouths stained by chewing betel nut.
I wrote in detail of my experiences,
    but I couldn't translate the stories
  etched on chipped and scratched faces.
Unable to find the language
    for things I could never know or grasp,
  I noted the poverty of my life at home.
Each country presenting itself for my privilege
    and me, not declaring my preconceptions at customs.

Eucharist under golden arches

All roads lead to this
most sacred of places
where millions worship
and miracles are made to order with fries.

In cars, bikes and rickshaws,
believers queue for the sacrament,
or at least a sugar high,
demanding more and more be packed
into wafer-thin attention spans.

After years of hosting birthday parties
and family dinners, it's like home,
but with more plastic.
The aromas of childhood wafting through
give crowds a taste of nostalgia
with added preservatives.

In the beginning,
the goal was to save the masses
from the ordeal of home cooked meals.
Now, it's to reach out to the world
and rescue the poor
from the temptations of rice.

Throughout, missionaries spread the word
that there will be burgers, fries and shakes for everyone.
There will be red and gold flags
on Everest, the pyramids, and Antarctica.
And there will be a clown
welcoming pilgrims at the pearly gates.

Memories in analogue

These memories are stored on vinyl:
first dog bite, last poo in the pants,
eating cheese and vegemite sandwiches.
I move the needle to an old favourite:
the squall of voices in a playground,
then wobbling on a bike down a quiet street.
The dust and crackle makes them authentic.

Others are stored on disc.
They replay on a digital screen.
But more often than not,
I delete the events of yesterday,
and I don't download my childhood –
its transmission is slow and fuzzy.
Instead, I return to the vinyl
and enjoy it while I can.
It doesn't matter how they're kept:
all memories stutter or jump when scratched.

stuck in the amusement parlour of unwanted memories

pac man gobbles up fruit
on the screen of your mind
you clear one level
knowing the next one will be harder
it's the usual pattern repeating
like the way a game of chasing death
turns into death chasing you
or the way the past stalks the present
and offers a future playing the same old roles

you try to change the system
and attack the memories
that close in like space invaders
but there are too many
to shoot down all at once

out of money and tokens
you steer the wheel of a driving demo
and pretend it's not a simulation
being caught again
loitering and chewing
on the bubble gum of existence

Unemployment haiku

If time is money
you're now stinking rich. You try
to spend it wisely.

At Cash Converters,
you sell your lifestyle for
less than half its worth.

At the check-out, you
wait with a basketful of
two-minute noodles.

At Centrelink, blank
and downward faces become
less strange over time.

Day time TV sucks
you in and becomes your
favourite addiction.

Your TV-induced
headaches are sponsored by your
former employer.

Each day without work
erodes your confidence in
the economy.

Feeling powerless
and angry about the time/
money ratio,

you beat the system,
cooking two-minute noodles
in one and a half.

Another makeover show

Rebels slash through jungle in Sierra Leone.
A renovation team invades a house in Sydney.

The rebels enter a clearing, and bullets fly.
The decorators move in wearing paint aprons.

Bodies lie in grass, covered in pixels.
In the backyard, a new water feature will bring energy.

A seven-year-old holds an AK47, looks right at the camera.
Stripping wallpaper is messy, but fun.

The rebels decide to evacuate their village.
The decorators can't decide between peach and lilac for the bathroom.

Women carry their possessions in baskets on their heads.
Well-placed ferns give good *feng shui*.

The women hold hands with children, already their backs to the camera.
The team is excited and ready to reveal their surprise.

Land mines and a three-day walk between the village and a refugee camp.
A blindfolded couple enters a bedroom, uncovers their eyes:

O
my
God

20 : 80

a cola brand's budget for advertising bulges over twelve african GDPs as six billion consumers squeeze fruit in the global supermarket one point two clear the shelves four point eight rummage for leftovers while searching for a cure for boredom researchers have discovered the number of grams of chocolate required to fill the emptiness of a western lifestyle is greater than or equal to the number of hours the average person spends pushing a shopping trolley over a lifetime decreases in the latest rates of happiness have reinforced fears the gap between those with and without is widening causing many to queue for handouts to calculate the value of cosmetic surgery worldwide just multiply the number of beggars by the number of land mines and divide by the number of missing limbs incoming reports from california confirm that you are unique the barcode tattooed on your genitalia distinguishes you from your clones in response to falling literacy levels popular magazines will publish only in the language of kilos and calories while dress size now determines success the wholesale theft of self esteem is not reported in tonight's news somewhere between a tax rise and the latest list of injured footballers tens of thousands die in an earthquake in a fourth world country as talkback lines overheat with angry taxpayers one resilient american kid delivers a tear to the eyes of millions

America

America, your humour doesn't always translate
into mass laughter. In other words,
your sitcoms give me the shits,
and I'm tired of watching those punch lines
roll in across the Pacific.
America, I hate to tell you,
your shows about losing weight in a boot camp:
they're not popular in Ethiopia.
The more you lose in pounds, the more you gain in confidence,
and, America, that's something you don't need more of.
Hi America, I'm the next American Idol.   *No, I am.*   *No, I am.*
I hear this year's Rwandan Idol won't be televised.
America, you see yourself as bold and beautiful,
but I know there's more to you
than perfect hair and perfect teeth.
You say your mind is free
even though you still believe
that heroes have American accents
while villains are marked by foreign inflections
and a love of bad moustaches.
America, you were the one voted most likely to succeed,
but who are you now?
John Wayne riding in the deserts
of Iraq, smiling one minute, killing the next?
Or an eccentric genius,
using the world as a theatre
for your dramas of crime and law at one end,
your games of war at the other?
America, will there be a *CSI Baghdad*?
I hear the next *Survivor*

is being filmed on Guantanamo Bay.
I hear the next Hollywood blockbuster
features A-list actors in uniform
and a CGI invasion of both Iran and Syria.
With all that bursting energy,
no wonder cheerleaders wave their pom-poms on the sidelines
even when you drop bombs on crowded cities.
But America, that narrative
of good versus evil is getting old,
and fans are turning away
faster than you can slap on
a happy ending.

Alert but not alarmed

After watching the news again and again, you imagine your own city flattened with fear. You imagine sirens compressing air, and people with eyes full of smoke staggering along main streets. And you imagine suburbs peppered with the shrapnel of politically-sponsored anxiety.

But from your front window there is only the quiet swirl of your mind's atmosphere. The city appears unchanged, yet, like the disappearance of frogs from mountain streams, you know something less visible, less newsworthy, is occurring. Unannounced, something causes your system to implode, and you enter a new era of pre-emption.

The official level of fear is raised to red. Alert but not alarmed, you analyse the words of experts, and a threat of attack begins to follow you through the streets. You cross a bridge, enter a government building, and wonder at what point a group becomes a crowd. Picking up friends from an airport that's smoke-free but reeks of oil fumes, you scan faces for signs of concern. You worry about loved ones in other cities and everyone in your neighbourhood. And you can't disconnect from the warnings that scroll through your mind.

The unfamiliar becomes familiar. After hearing your heart's techno-beat all day and night for months, you realise on heightened anxiety, anticipation is the killer. You begin to second-guess your own intelligence information. You learn to make choices based on percentages, and see that everywhere there's risk. The supermarket seems safe, except for the four-wheel-drives circling the car park. You realise some dangers lose their aura: driving on a country road brings freedom not fear. And you keep living, knowing your favourite food has more in it than just junk, knowing the person driving towards you could be drunk.

Instead of watching the news, you unimagine politicians appearing in your living room at night, you unimagine the fruits of foreign policy and the plans of future martyrs going underground, you unimagine the rhetoric that disguises aggression as liberation, and you unimagine the private grief that's not reported. You unimagine these things until they become a distant murmur; until you hear once again dogs barking in the neighbourhood and crickets warning of rain; until you rediscover the mosaic existence of everyday life.

In search of news that's free of the press, you drive to the coast and watch the stars from a swag on the sand. You hear the ocean snoring all night, and wake to see packs of surfers marking their territory. You avoid surf politics and negotiate waves closer to shore, but the random surge forces you into the ocean's culture. Demonstrating the struggle between power and resistance, its ancient rhythms push and bend your body, leaving you on your knees with a mouthful of salt. And you sit on the sand, face the horizon, knowing only what you see – one moment tumbling into the next.

A relationship with fear

Fear sits in the front row and heckles when you speak in public.
    Fear loiters around the train station at night.
        Fear joins you on a long flight
    and annoys you with nervous chatter.
Fear walks into a crowded room at the same time as you,
    and you discover mutual interests.
        Fear doesn't believe in coincidence, and neither do you.
    Feeling more comfortable with fear than with others,
you start spending time together.
    Fear listens during the long and lonely hours,
        sharing quiet moments while the city sleeps.
    Before long, you're using the language of 'us' and 'them'
and finishing each other's sentences.
    Though there's conflict, you can't bear to be apart.
        So fear moves in for good.
    Gradually, you start to see another side of fear.
After a few drinks one night, fear becomes aggressive
    and puts you down in front of others.
        Fear hangs around the house all day,
    wanting to know all your movements.
Jealous of you going out with friends,
    fear confronts you in a dark alley of the mind,
        saying the world is dangerous,
    but the 'unknown' is worse.

Fear tells you that government policy makes sense,
   that razor wire should be everywhere.
      You express a need for space,
   but fear says you can't cope on your own.
One day fear locks all the doors and won't let you out of the house.
    One day you come home and find fear curled in a foetal position.
     One day fear disappears and doesn't return for months.
  You hear a rumour that fear has found someone else.
Then one day fear arrives at your doorstep, begging to be let back in.

zooming in

over there

beyond the botanic gardens

to the left of the mall

just right of the freeway

nah   not as far as the train station

near the government building

that crane   yeah

just in front of it

down the bottom

further down

along the graffitied wall

keep going

yeah the industrial bin

behind it there

under that flattened cardboard box

there   see

there's someone there

Unlicensed, Barrier Highway

At 140 Ks, To remove the subject from the poem, begin by removing the first person
with one hand from the car, the car from the bitumen, the bitumen from the dirt.
on the wheel, You might notice a residual presence – the landscape changed by
the other tyre prints – and the traces of images stolen by the unfocussed eye.
writing on scraps So, start again. Construct a new 'self' from the scraps of paper
of paper, on the passenger seat. Personify yourself: make it more animate than
inspiration booms you really are. Neatly tie a metaphor in a watertight carry bag.
through an open window. Take your 'self' away from everything you know. Think
But again, of all the languages dying from neglect, and your own: more
like the illusion pervasive than McDonald's. Passing 'Dead Man's Creek', you
of water on bitumen, imagine a spaghetti-western being filmed. As a gendered
images are too elusive space where death is present, it's more than a creek that's
to be captured been dry for years. Here, drought is the fifth season. Everything's
and hung out to dry relative. The phrase 'just past Broken Hill' refers to a space
on paper. somewhere between Adelaide and Sydney, Peterborough and Wilcannia.
What is empty From here to the nearest town, is it 200 Ks, 2 hours or 2 sunsets
to me is full of life rounded up to the nearest sunrise? How long does it take for an
to someone else. image to move from horizon to eye to brain to paper, measured
There must be reptiles in milliseconds, metres, feet, iambs? Meaning is held for a
sliding under ancient rocks. moment in a million-year-old wind, then dispersed by
I scan the horizon a southerly. All around is fluid: even you. So too, the line
for a sign, between road and desert, state and country; the Murray, like the
for an essence Mekong, straddles borders. Your day is structured more by events
of place. than numbers. A series of choices: Classic FM or local AM. Choosing
Is it the sun grazing strings and violins, you hear the sounds of woods, alps and
on red sand? streams, but see salt bush and semi-desert. The road is linear;
The straight lines your mind is not. You drive on – going back thousands of years
that graph the map not hundreds – bypassing Mozart, Marx, and so on. You picture
of a fatigued mind? wooden instruments: sticks clicking in neither 6/8 or 4/4
The kangaroo, emu vernacular? but to the pulse of cicadas. And you think if ever

Or is it the road kill,
the churning stomach,
the smell of a recent death,
a gathering of crows,
and a killer on the loose?

you position in present tense departure and arrival,
past and future, so a distant patch of earth becomes your
new home; if ever a trace of organic dust no longer
derives knowledge; if ever you mix history and pleasure
without a tinge of guilt: *remove my footprints, my body.*

words free

Simone G Matthews

Simone G Matthews loves reading and writing
poetry, fiction, biography and across the genre
explorations. She is writing her first novel,
Malinowski's Course. Autobibliographies as part of her
PhD studies under the supervision and mentorship
of Marion May Campbell.

Simone believes that reading and writing a poem can
help you unveil the interconnectedness beyond
words. Reading a poem can help you open up and
participate in something that seems impossible or
unknown and rewards you with an immense feeling
of shared freedom. From this point of view, the
following poems belong to you much more than to
the one who, in the end, only did the writing.

Acknowledgements

I acknowledge with gratitude that my writing is always under the influence and in dialogue with readings from Nicole Brossard, Adrienne Rich, Roland Barthes, J Borges, Christina Rossetti, E A Poe, F Garcia Lorca, G Stein, Paul Celan, Ezra Pound, T S Eliot, S Plath, Mallarme, Hafiz, Genet, Cixous and many others.

Poems in this collection have appeared and/or are under publication for *antiThesis, Strange 3, New Antigone, Talk Fiction. Proceedings of the Talk Fiction Postgraduate Creative Writing Colloquium* and *Friendly Street Poetry Reader 30.*

I am very indebted to Marion May Campbell for believing in my writing before even knowing me and for her infinite generosity in always sharing everything she knows about the mysterious world that reflects back to us from beyond the words.

for God to forgive a slow learner in giving back
for bibi, buni and ghita as they are always with me
for naomi, anthony and patricia for their love
for zia and nono for their warm care
for marion for her sharing, initiation and friendship
for mona, maria and florin
for csilla and zsuzsa
for anthony again and always as he is part of me
and for God who listened and spared his life

"I know this by the words I am missing . . . "
Nicole Brossard, Museum of Bone and Water

Contents

brief guide to slam poetry

because christina rossetti says:
i plucked pink blossoms from mine apple-tree
and wore them all that evening in my hairs
because adrienne rich says:
i came to explore the wreck. the words are purposes
because nicole brossard says:
language will reproduce with you in the folds of skin
this endless version of your body from now on unalterable
because they all perform
in this never ending slam difficult
to bear in one heart avid audience
turning page after page

there is still thin ice
for every woman who writes
there is still a ladder and no masks
to wear
for every woman who reads

the talking strips you bare

you are the navigator
with bubbling melancholic eyes
you try to find the street
the dwelling
any direction would do
driving through the metropolis
wasn't meant to be exhausting
but fun
take the south road
then we look out for indicators
i drive hoping to find the place
while you munch on your burger
we could just decide one
day against driving and talking
that strips us so bare

the androgynous scale[1]

how to reach there, where you cannot do otherwise than touch one's lips with
yours, just for a second, how could that be done, felt, thought, desired

how to miss the translation and not feel the need for it, for what you vaguely
remember as a masticating body-soul, intro-specting or speculating, labelled
commonly understanding, as a broken bridge between territories? When your
words are not interpreting in your own code what you mean, when you have
only the form, the sound of the other's speech without understanding it, just
like a veil that mummifies your body ... Isn't this a sign itself that you must
leave, that the whole relations are expunging you as abnormality, strange
corpus? Isn't this a warning when mirroring tunnels fold back into rays, than
petals, until you and the void change clothes and nakedness
you choose what is left of nakedness, the smoke of intersecting fissures.

they will say is because of Henry and look for a suicide note. Women have done
it, in many ways, men have done it too. Unreciprocated love, one gets the kiss,
the marriage and the other imagines the jump, so many times in so many ways,
angles, until the decision becomes fluid, part of one's body and one jumps off.
Through. Out of her, no noun should follow when your grammar dissolves,
expands. From a fishing net to an invisible diagram, until the limit of seeing,
clouds grasping the abyss of your eye, your self expanding in its jump
becoming it, absorbed by the layers of air, one with the whole, getting rid of the
framing, of the bordering body-soul

who is *you*, telling a story of *me*? Do you think it's a game, the imagining, the guessing of who I was, and why and what I did? Do you think you will get away with it and you won't pay for it even if you find the entry through the metaphors of my poems, the aperture almost ingested by the lines of my own fiction and diary and research?

when you cross latitudes, longitudes of different spaces, do you think you will reach in the right spot, where I was? And then, could you start with how, how to do it, the intersexing, the acknowledging of the androgynous scale.

the bracket or the space that lays out the scene: this was Maria Czaplicka's introspection before she took the decision to suicide. The writer reads her diary, her research notes on Aboriginal Siberia. The writer – a translator, a shaman to enter. Rituals, what, to impede the disaster at the end of the story. Notes.

in my imaginary space, she could escape the tragic exit
she could come back through a reverse ritual in imagining
she could continue to do what she has done best
(how? how to do it).

1 Fragment from 'Lamentations' in *Malinowski's Course. Autobibliographies*

hugh jackman

leave you alone
to watch the movie
the x-men van helsing
they all are on
your plate
crossing the mall
short and old
you forget to buy gluten-free flour
from the health food store
she will be angry
then
she will be leaving you
alone
to watch
the swordfish don't worry
she is the real victim
and has no where to go

poet unknown

poem read
at friendly street poets
in adelaide 2004
september 22
people laughed
people clapped their hands
poet unknown

poem read
at melbourne poets' union
april 4
people laughed
people clapped their hands
poet unknown

this morning you read
in the paper
(this is the old phrase becoming idiotically
a metaphor for checking the news online)
poet unknown
found dead

becoming written

"here I am, an old man in a dry month,
being read to by a boy, waiting for rain . . ."

T.S. Eliot, Gerontion

After the trip of life what trip shall I take
The boat is out
The house looks like a boat too . . .

I have to clear this thought away
Like a chocolate bar before it melts

I have to try not to get dizzy again and hold on something
That is real and precise and conventionally normal:

She wants a chocolate cake
That's all she wants

The boat is out and waves will gently shove it away
Before its image melts in the dark
I must take another trip
Before this one will be finished

spring

i don't want to be sexual
with you and i don't want
you to get embarrassed
while
i walk naked on the streets

i don't want to be nagging
and new age with you
i don't want you to blush and
run away
while
i shout that i love you
at tony 'n mark' s fruit market
or at least
this is my plan
to touch spring's nose again

me the bellyflopped, you the papermate

we count our heroes
…

because we don't know their names
we don't know what food they like
whom they love
and if they drive sedan or smoke
or buy flowers for their mothers
if they enjoy the football or the cricket

between me the bellyflopped
and you the papermate
we count our heroes
shouldn't
we
just
jump
save
them
from drowning?

oyster bar

you are dreaming
of one hour stress free
eating oysters kilpatrick
and drinking a glass of seaview

you are squeezing this dream
eggwhites slippering through your fingers
between picking-up rosie
from school
and feeding tim-tim

cars can pass you by
fragments of looking at you – people
and commercials questioning you
can pass you by
you just focus hanging in there and focus
on what is next
to do
be careful though to keep your
target receipt
just in case they don't fit him

target 100% happy

monsters' story

no money today
at atm

another long weekend
yes you know the drill
just use your imagination
tell her a story with monsters
eating everything in the
fridge
other than a slice of bread
and homebrand strawberry jam
who are they?

she always asks
about the monsters
in leather
and purple blue slippers
drinking all the milk
and orange juice

look mummy
they left some
arnott teddy bears alive

how to rewind this event
paraphrasing Poe's Scythe of Time

while walking through the reading mall
men were talking
women were screaming
children were choking

you see zenobia
in her d&g t-shirt
and orange sun-glasses
talking, screaming, having coffee with poe

while walking through the reading mall
you see poe, in his black coat,
smoking cigarette after cigarette (which coffee shop
is that in year 2005, southern hemisphere smoke-free earthsea?)

in the middle of the mall
a jazz band in the middle of the jazz band
diana with hair in her eyes
sings and dances
dances and sings
she screams towards you
your head falls off too much reading,
less living

how to rewind this event, Mr Poe?

making scenes

"each partner of a scene dreams of having the last word.
To speak last, 'to conclude', is to assign a destiny to
everything that has been said, is to master, to possess,
to absolve, to bludgeon meaning ..."

Roland Barthes, *A Lover's Discourse*

— un-city them, these women
— *no one has imagined us*[1]
from oak or rock
black and white, echoes from the womb,
— *i am returning.*
let me return to my spring of water![2]
— i am trembling in the white tub
and slide deep and deeper into the wavy water
there is no time left to find the wrinkles
and no eyes left to read between the flakes of steam
just plain happiness of returning there
again

— *let us take the air, in a tobacco trance,*
admire the monuments,
discuss the late events,
correct our watches by the public clocks.
then sit for an half an hour and drink our bocks[3]
— leave me alone on a saturday evening
on one of these streets
an old lady offers me a smile — 'the sunset is beautiful,
isn't it?' her hands are young, her nails red polished

leave me alone on this saturday evening
from the cement sidewalk
i can still see her waving towards me
and it is not raining
and i am not depressed and i am not worried for
not cleaning the house
not responding to your mum's invitation of going to dinner
not doing what i am expected to do, to say, to think
i am not worried just alone
incorrectly alone

*– please spice, please no name, place a whole weight, sink
into a standard rising . . .*[4]
– never his pain more painful for me
never his ascending more giving, his return more immediate
i read this verse
and i feel new

*– for god, our god is a gallant foe
that playeth behind the veil*[5]
– let's unpack,
do you have time to help me unpack?

the trip was long and longer it seems for you
as you are older
and wiser but that is no excuse
how can you rest if all you have it's
crowded in a bag . . .
how can you claim 'this is all about reaching here, with you'?

— tunes in to light's pitch: there are
still songs to be sung on the other side
of mankind[6]

— for mum told you not to use makeup
and perfume and cool clothes
not to be afraid of what you cannot accept
she has asked you not to laugh at people that are
unaware of themselves
not to write poems
not to cross the line
but you had to see
you had to try living inside your poem like a homeless
and all made sense: streets were as they should be: not usual faces
but greater and lesser poets,
for mum told you not to cross the line
whoever steps over it she never comes back
only the reflection in god's tear
remains to flicker a yawn
— i don't listen to you grandma

— for i have known them all already, known them all
have known the evenings, mornings, afternoons,
i have measured out my life with coffee spoons[7]

— you used to say:
"don't keep looking at me with those big brown eyes!"
and still, i don't listen to you grandma
you used to say: "do whatever you want to do,
but don't end like me: between one dishwashing
and the next"

what i read and what i write doesn't measure out my life
what i cook and what i wash
what i work and whom i help
what i give and
whom i love
rhythmically and slowly
swallows the girl with big brown eyes

– mutely like the jaws of the city – catwalks de-composing –
we believe we are immortals
and nothing will stop this living, spontaneous
daring living no need to leave anything behind

– *what is this, behind this veil, is it ugly, is it beautiful?*[8]
– we are feeling sleepy and feverish
and try to hide behind spirals of food and drinks
we believe in
not leaving behind a trace
a poem a painting a discovery with no sins
those who left something behind
are mute like the jaws of these women half men half veils

– *here i am, an old man in a dry month,*
being read to by a boy, waiting for rain . . .[9]

– i have to clear this thought away
like a chocolate bar before it melts
i have to try not to get dizzy again and hold on something,
that is, real and precise and conventionally normal
– she wants a chocolate cake
that's all she wants

– can you hear this comma as i read it?[10]
– everything in the world will end in a book
this is how they have translated the question
maybe
you are a letter and your life is the word in the middle of a sentence if
you could finish it,
so you are this black mark
and you love many people and hate less
and you give yourself to everybody as reward for they are alive
maybe i am this comma, almost inverted wings above
seven wheels crossing the road if i could finish it
and i love many people and hate less

– think about this,
this great pull in us to connect[11]
– the one of me that lives
i don't know much of her i just see her sometimes and alone
the one of me that will live in the future
i know her even less and she's always sad always vague
the one of me that lived
is my best friend:
she visits me often and helps me and listens
she is never alone, always with somebody – true happiness

bare feet – true happiness
– it's winter for me summer for you
bare feet guided to another world
my mum said 'it's ok, you leave, you'll see different,
you'll know different, don't be afraid of the city'
it's winter for me summer for you
my mum is sliding away in a smoking sphere

— everything happens nothing is remembered
in those dimensioned cabinets of glass . . .[12]
– if only *my* memories would be a warm blanket
to keep all of you from passing away
alive

— for this discovery of yours will create forgetfulness in the learners' souls,
    because they will not use their memories[13]
– your face reflects hundreds of faces
everybody with impertinence with obstinacy with shyness and beauty
with love and with hate blame the letters,
blame the letters, if that makes you happy

– the poet should speak about what we know only for ourselves
– *he* should use speech and *she* should be a spectator
and *it* should be able to use the spectacles – that is the image,
(*if they heard the truth even from oak or rock it was enough for them*[14])

that is the convention
that you will find and break
as you go out of the scene
— you have an eye, it's an image.[15]

All quotes from *The Norton Anthology of Poetry*, WW Norton & Company, 5th edition, 2004

1 Adrienne Rich, *Twenty-one Love Poems*, I
2 Federico Garcia Lorca, *The Known Way*
3 TS Eliot, *Portrait of a Lady*
4 G Stein, *Tender Buttons, Food*
5 Ezra Pound, *Ballad for Gloom*
6 Paul Celan, *Thread Suns*
7 TS Eliot, *Prufock*
8 Sylvia Plath, *A Birthday Present*

9 TS Eliot, *Gerontion*
10 G Mallarme, *Manuscript*
11 Hafiz, *With that moon language*
12 JL Borges, *Mirrors*
13 Socrates in *Plato, Phaedrus*
14 Socrates in *Plato, Phaedrus*
15 Sylvia Plath, *The Applicant*

perfect flowers

an intersext[1] that doesn't want to be a poem in prose

i write because i look for an opening
a fissure between realities and imaginaries to defy time, the exhausting, the non-aging, the infinite linearity
every story i hear or read brings my past back to me memories are past belongings and knowing this, could you ever resist narrative? i am too curious, too longing for my *others* locked in loops of stories that become alive at the trigger of other stories
it (the storytelling) is never ending
yours and mine, the listening, the reading or even the writing are rhythmically limited by the aging body

poetry, you say gives us the shivers, the furies, the unhappiness
poetry comes with her intense dreaming and living from a time that didn't happen as yet at her weakest point is *déjà vu* she comes from other worlds and takes you and me with her, and as young as she walks side by side with us, older than narrative, she's the great grandmother cradling a crying baby with pure sounds

*

my next book is going to be about you, you reading helen garner's "civilization and its discontents",
it will tell the story of how you decided to make this painting about a wild woman and her giving birth
but first i will have to open other books and research so that i understand your intentions, otherwise how could you distinguish biography from fiction? freud's "civilization and its discontents" is one reading you recommend and you leave me with the guessing, imagining, dreaming, writing beyond expectations and reading

52

this is the blossoming circle that you and me, and us on the other hand we are
caught in

*

at this moment i can share with you the title, *perfect flowers*, reality and
metaphor simultaneously
roses and viburnums have perfect flowers and the language playfully as it sounds
is always right
we call them *perfect* because each flower has both stamens and pistil, both sexes,
apples, plums, tomatoes and many ornamental flowers, all of them plants with
perfect flowers
the others, the unlucky ones, we call them dioecious
their male flowers appear on one plant and female flowers on another

*

we are too shy to admit, bearing a round ripe shyness before the poetry and
prose dispute,
when chromosomes and cultural pressures perform a binary cheat, shouldn't
your heart tell you what you are?

*

we are dioecious, and from inside a dioecious room, everything outside in the
garden seems less perfect
it's the language that helps us remember what we call perfect
but we don't want to remember
our discontent shamefully addressing the sick ones, abnormal ones, the IT as we
abbreviate the intersexed and transgendered

*

it happened in our family in the last weeks or so
claire has given birth to a baby-boy
lily had a miscarriage *mislife* would say more about the tragic event

the mother had to accept that the five-month baby is going to take the breath of
death yellow roses were smiling in the vase, on claire's bedside,
yellow roses were in tears on a sympathy card that lily has left behind at the
hospital
she walked out, she had to
between life and mislife, there was a poem of pain winking to God

*

boys and girls
i listen to your explanation (of what happens parallel to our conversation in
helen garner's short story) and dream of a writing humble enough not to want
classification, a writing outside the genre, a writing without the gender
is it possible to be such a writing or to have such a writing
girls and boys

*

this is what you need, a good women laughter
only that laughter would dissolve your outrage with God of letting your baby
die
you could take Demeter's part in the story of *Baubo: The Belly Goddess*[2]
if only you would go and see a medicine woman
you could smile of Baubo, the dancing deformed goddess, that had no head but
her nipples were her eyes and her vulva – her mouth
her dirty dancing and jokes made Demeter laugh and by laughing she renewed
her energies
maybe you could have the book and read the story yourself
you could find yourself laughing and forgetting about blaming
is that what baubo teaches us, that our body-souls are perfect flowers? *Laugh-
with-humility*

the place is naked abandoned and angry with a nosy nail
I will hang a mirror there
and under it *You are what you read*

1 "For if texts are sexed, might the same not be true about the *intersexts?* Are there sexual implications to different ways of relating texts to each other? To coin a new word, are not different *intersexts* possible?(. . .)" Hanrahan, Mairead, 'Genet and Cixous: The InterSext', *The French Review*, Vol. 72, No. 4. (Mar., 1999), pp. 719–729.

2 C Pinkola Estes, *Women Who Run With Wolves*, 1998, Random House, Australia, pp. 337–338.

noise and haste

the last page
is about you
the last page of a book is like the last words of a person before she or he passes
away, you may try to look at this book as if it would be a person, to better see
this person in front of your eyes, until it stands closer to you, 'it' so that gender
doesn't imprison

the writer, one of the soul's guests, inappropriately sometimes called 'the
author', is just a medium, in the same way as a hypnotized patient would
talk long hours about things, people, stories, real and borrowed echoes of
an estranged imagination
(you may think this is just an allegory, in a similar way that wisdom was
portrayed as a young maid in the garden of misery, a painting you have
seen reproduced on a website)

when i understood that my mother was going to die,
i was on the phone with her and she barely was breathing, struggling for
the fullness of words,
over the phone, thousands and thousands of miles away, at the other end
of the world, *not understanding,*

but feeling the pain, the impossibility of erasing that gap, eliminating the
cities, the seas, and the impassive mountains and hills, millions of people
between me reaching her,
thousands of air particles savouring their displacement with sarcasm and
just be there with her, i tried to kill the tears with a voice and told her
that i loved her and that her granddaughter loved her too and there were
fractions when i could feel the candles vanishing with the cruelty and
softness of a strange forgotten language,

of what i could possibly not say,
not just put in words, but give her as light as a feather in a sound as
keeping her hand in my hand could have been, warm and close,
something to help her when passing, when facing away,
that i would love and do everything she would do, in the way she would
only do it, for my daughter, that's what i discovered in the act of saying,
giving in to drops of
noise and haste that i could hear, she would touch them one by one
snowflakes on her lips, straining for a last time to give shape to the
threads of thought vibrating out of her heart all her living powers in
broken wording, newly born sounds "... so much"

this is how it ends, you measuring in the sunflower of your eyes the figure
of it,
its living from the beginning to the end, emotions and thoughts, stories
and connections, proof for it's alive and breathing and that only when
terribly alive you earn a right to pass away,
in passing away or *through*

through is the word for how it ends,
like a fruit nurturing its kernel,
you might find peeling away its skin,
savouring the layers of ink and pulp,
tired of chasing its guest of flesh and blood

female change

it	you open this door
is	is the light tearing them apart
a	in the mouth-mirrors?
veiled	they're soaking ashamed afraid
woman	not healthy not young
half-	you forget the look
dreamed	you change
little	knowing this by shivering, aborting
birds	missing words

from *Selected Poems by Anais Nin and Other See-Saw Translations*

jars of artefacts

Rachel Manning

Rachel Manning was born and raised in South Australia. She studied Literature and Education at Flinders University before travelling widely. She currently works as an adult educator.

She has been writing poetry since the age of 10, when her first poem was stuck up on the wall of her Year 3 classroom. She got a taste for publication and has since been widely published in South Australia and nationally.

Rachel is currently working on another collection of poems and her first novel.

Acknowledgements

Adelaide Review for 'archaeology'
Friendly Street for 'cleansing', 'pixel nervosa',
'the other woman' and 'scene change'
Page Seventeen for 'etiquette'
Pendulum for 'cataracts'

For Nic, whose love, support and
encouragement helped bring my poetry out
from where it was hiding.

Contents

cataracts

earlier

grandmother had cataracts
in both eyes
yet still saw well enough
to comment on
the dust
in my lounge room

the doctor removed the eyes
rolled them around on her cheeks
then popped them back in

later

the yellowed patch was peeled back
taking bits of skin and hairs

grandfather leaned in for a look

she saw clearly at last
and cried in frightened delight
arthur
oh dear
arthur
how old and ugly you have grown

quickly
bring me a mirror

seconds

you grill me over pasta
question over wine
judge over coffee

despite the ritual
of careful circling
and surmising intention
the table is cleared

common threads
of interest
prove a taste
of friendship

still early days
as you scan the menu
for seconds

archaeology

this was a week of digging

we moved barrow-loads of
that time we went to the movies
i coarse-sieved piles of
that look on your face when we danced
you rinsed down shovels full of
the plates i used when you came to dinner

we pegged out
grid-lines in time

unearthed
first meeting

measured
first date

pinned out
first fuck

we used
fine-haired brushes
tweezers
pins

we
extracted
exhumed
labelled
categorised
preserved

now

jars of artefacts
line our lives

evidence of

ancient
civilisation

proof of

perfect
heathenry

first draft

i roll your flesh
in my mind's typewriter
and tap ink-wet words of lust

      across your breasts
      across your thighs

each carriage return induces gasps
each tabulation groans
as poetry flows from inside you

      a first draft
      past my lips

etiquette

the etiquette of close quarters
my new lovers' house

does my coffee belong on a coaster
should my shoes be left in the lounge
do my cigarette butts lie easily in the geraniums

i consider the options of
        placement
        position
        propriety

the minefield of choice
        in a delicately balanced dance
        of civility
        and displays of house-training skill

while animals shed
confusion and hair
in twisted underwear
discarded in lust

sucked and tucked

she checked in
       checked out
let it all hang out
went for it big time
       finally

she got measured up
       marked out
pre-paid the lot
chose the after shot
       carefully

she got opened up
       stretched out
probed up
and scraped out
       entirely

she got signed out
       pimped about
picked up and put out
'til her debts were paid
       categorically

cleansing

i vacuum the bedroom as you
sort pack and leave

each stroke sucks chunks of
memory regret and loss

i vacuum first feelings of
love fear and desire

i sweep sleepless nights of
tension silence and glances

i scrub courting rituals of
words touch and lust

i polish virginal pangs of
caress stroke and kiss

i scour first discoveries of
fingers mouth and breast

i keep the dust bag
i know i should empty

these women

these women
draw together threads
from forgotten land mines
and
burnt out synagogues
glistening with swastikas
and
refugees who peer through
diamond nets of wire

       these women
       weave a blanket of hope
       and drape it across
       the shoulders of our children

these women
draw together pulp
of old growth rainforest
and
the forty-four species that existed
when we went to bed last night
but
somehow between then and waking
just stopped being

these women
sew a quilt of love
and wrap it warmly
around our children

these women
dance between
double lanes of traffic
and
pits filled with
plastic bags and sump oil
and
they marvel at the world
as the sun bleeds through clouds

these women
knit a jumper of faith
and pull it gently over the
outstretched arms of our children

these women
step out from behind
the flags and the desires
and
grow a future
from
this now

us and them

i sweat in your garden
scrape cuttings into piles
sneeze dust that's blown
around your ivy for years

       memories of women
       frolic in your hedges

i rearrange your furniture
drag floorboards into view
expose masonry scarring
hidden by arrangement

       they stop the gaps
       behind your skirtings

i catch myself reflected
by dull globes and glances
i see me watching you
watching me seeing me

       they skip by your
       uncurtained windows

i lie in your arms
and breathe your smile

       afraid of joining them

grasmere

bill
i visited your town of choice
i promise you
you would not choose it now

entrepreneurs offer
t-shirts inscribed
"i wandered lonely as a cloud"
or a coffee mug
tea towel
pen
bookmark
chocolate bar
thimble
teaspoon
jumper
whatever

spoons

your nape traces shape
across my sight
a fault-line ridged
sunset silhouette
against streetlights
and moon

your ears reverse
into the oncoming traffic
of my highway vision
i check shoulders
for the potatoes
mums always warn of

no self-sown undergrowth
taints your vegetable patch

your gold chain writhes
though nape canyon
the colorado
on a good day
unravaged by panners
and dredgers

and I lie
a bed-time
away

knowing that
woman cannot live
on potatoes alone

time

the mantel clock freezes
mid-tick
the paper pauses
at the peak of its
verandah-bound arc

and you are all
that's left
of time
a rhythmic sleep
of
sunday morning
dreams

pixel nervosa

your digital camera
allows your eating disorder
to soar to new heights

you capture food in pixels
create jpegs of your breakfast
  bitmaps of lunch
  gifs of dinner

your pc's menu
takes on
an entirely new meaning

later
you binge
in a slideshow of courses
meals flash across your screen
in
calorific technicolour

you savour each morsel
as it slips
  past
  and down
  and through

you're fit to burst
stretched to server capacity
temporarily sated

until
remorse sets in
and
the download begins

at ten megabytes per minute
it takes seventeen seconds
to move the entire contents
of your stomach
to the recycle bin

sleeper

your dream-heavy
glottal stops
    rich with
    toothpasted
    garlic
draw me from then

sleep takes cover
hiding beneath
    blanketed
    whispers
    in darkness
cocooned by desire

distant
backyard murmuring
nudges rhythm
    you turn
    over away
    from me
into darkness

still
i guard from behind
constant patrol
    ensures
    i ease
    your eyes
from tangled shadows

planet man

at first
i mistook your speech
for
peaceful contemplation

until
i noticed your wall of teeth
damning
anger within

at first
i mistook your politics
for
small L liberal likenesses

until
i heard your rousing oration
on
the hanging of other

at first
i mistook your solitude
for
thinking time and solace

until
i realised no one liked you

not even you

the other woman

i grasp the life jackets you offer
        calls that ring in my hallway
        flowers that fill my lounge

i cling to them in frenzy
and confront myself with options
        hold on
        hoping your ship will collect me
        let go
        peacefully and silently slip under

i thrash about
panic when i loosen my grip
afraid of the cold darkness
my only achievement to date
has been the attraction of sharks

        i wish i were a stronger swimmer
        i wish you were a better navigator

perversely i'm glad we're not
in this current
i don't have to make a choice

i can reserve my flares
for another wreck

the last post

your letter invades
my day of distractions
a hypodermic shot
of indiscretions past

        historic toxins
        wash within
        these needle
        hardened arteries

better your cold turkey line
        than this overdose of lies

spliffed

with what to say
in sleeping haze
of exhaustion
and hash

profound words
once pooled within
seep slowly away
till spent balloons

and cigarette butts
dotted like
strawberries on
a step

are all that
remain

white horses
chalk mines
and death

pervade dreams
of australia
and people
cease to exist

i stopped dreaming
of her
and weights
lifted

goad

graven image
grave image
gray
engrave image
enslave image
stay
form image
inform image
now
pray image
play image
pay

scene change

i bought tickets to the opera
but before i had the chance
to surprise you with a program
you drew the curtain mid overture

       we rehearsed together years
       performed together months
       before you decided upon
       your character's new face

i went to the premiere alone
our debut filled my senses
at every cue
every aside

and still
a season later
each line of that offstage scene
sends my memory falling
into choruses of tragedy

opening night sell out
second scene change

perfectly delivered lines
timely props and cues
every gesture divine
as each rehearsal
had been endlessly
imagined

      inevitable cancellation
      inexplicably premature

she quit
re-wrote the ending
to create this
one-woman show
this travelling circus

      sell
      out

paris-ite

rodin's reflection pool
froze over this morning
the thinker got chilblains
the kissers' lips stuck together

      this parisian christmas
      lined with fresh baguettes
      and fresher dog shit
      fills my nostrils to overflowing

not until i reached the top
survived the cattle run of queues
struggled to eiffel's peak
did my camera's battery die

      my imagination discovers
      the eighth law
      of gravitational physics

a fifty franc lithium battery
falls at exactly the same rate
as a fully clothed french pre-schooler

      less messy though
      by half

foreign phrases

i studied esperanto at uni
interested not in language
but the teacher who was
the most beautiful man on earth

i studied esperanto for months
before the shocking realisation
i was in love with a classmate
the most beautiful woman on earth

i quit esperanto immediately
those foreign phrases
were not for me

painting by numbers

your fingers play with
space and time

hours flow
from your lips

five days drip by
in the holes
between
my breaths

planets dislodge
and skid

galaxies snail in
upon themselves

and still we
paint by numbers

two lifetimes of
colour two

farewell nepal

according to the pseudo-scientific documentary
aired on a return flight from sydney last week
the entire continent of india
      (please ensure your tray table is safely stowed)
moves northward by fifteen centimetres
      (please ensure your seat is returned to the upright position)
every year

butting into asia
crushing mountain upon mountain
and making headway of
fifteen centimetres
every single year
      that's six inches in the old language
           the height of a pint
                the width of an octave
                    the length of a prayer

at this rate by the year ten million
      one hundred and forty seven thousand
           two hundred and eleven
           a.d.
nepal will have ceased to exist

and
mt everest will have officially slipped into
the administrative subdivision of
the people's republic of china

the communist plot thickens

Friendly Street New Poets Series